Mind Wanders

Veerle Rutten

BookLeaf
Publishing

India | USA | UK

Presentation by *BookLeaf Publishing*

Web: www.bookleafpub.com

E-mail: info@bookleafpub.com

ISBN: 9789357449113

First edition 2022

DEDICATION

For those who stayed.

ACKNOWLEDGEMENT

I want to thank everyone who made my fight worth it and who has helped me through my darkest times, because of you I chose to live; because of you I am still here.

Mind

And how I wish
my mind was a little less
hectic

A little less
messed up

A little less
dark

And how I wish
my mind was a little more
calm

A little more
clean

A little more
colorful

Prisoner

I cannot quite escape
this place
my mind made a maze

barely room to breathe
prisoned by my own thoughts
and too blinded
to see the light
within myself

She

She put a little light
back into my eyes
to help me see the world
a little brighter

Peace

I am not
nor was I ever
okay
with losing you

but it also
brought
so much
peace

Ironic

Isn't it ironic
how you,
almost in tears,
begged me
not to give up on you
like everyone else did
only for you
to give up on me
in the end

Is that why you left?

I saw the universe
when I looked into
your eyes.

Yet the only thing
you saw in my eyes
was sadness

Sometimes relapse is needed

I begged to God
not to have a relapse again
little did I know
relapse was needed
to see how stuck
in progress
I really was

I fell in love

And between
all of our
phone calls,
random jokes
and all of our laughs
I started to imagine
a future with you

It's just my mind messing with me

Sometimes
when I close my eyes
I can see you again

it's like you're standing
in front of me
and I can touch you

but then,
when I open my eyes
you are gone.
And I can't see clear anymore,
because of the tears
filled up in my eyes

The night you left

My lungs kept asking
for some fresh air
but I had to press
my pillow
against my mouth
because I couldn't stop crying
and I didn't want to make a sound

My heart

My heart doesn't beat faster anymore
when I am with you
It doesn't skip a beat
when my eyes meet yours
and I guess it was then
when I realized
how much I love you
because my soul has found
its peace
when I am with you

Burning

I kept rereading
our story

and rereading
and rereading

but the ending
did not change
so I burned the book

Toxic relationships

I used to be afraid
of losing you
but it took losing you
to realize how much
I needed to lose you

Losing you

I have already forgotten
the sound of your voice
and the sound of your laugh
I have forgotten some parts
of our memories
I have lost you
and I keep losing you
over and over again

Hurricane Depression

There's a hurricane in my head,
destroying the good that's left inside of me
making my head a terrible mess

There's no sun in my head
to reveal what's been broken
or still standing tall

Evenings & Nights

I spent evenings and nights
silently crying in my bedroom,
telling myself that I had to hold on
just a little while longer
because we would turn out fine,
if only I gave it a little more time

I spent evenings and nights
silently writing in my bedroom
telling myself that if I kept writing,
the pain will disappear,
becoming words on this page

I spent evenings and nights
silently thinking in my bedroom
telling myself I should stop
this overthinking

I spent evenings and nights
silently sitting in my bedroom
with a mind that didn't shut up
putting every bad thing on repeat

I spent evenings and nights
silently sitting in my bedroom
holding a blade between my fingers
wanting to kill the pain of missing you
with physical pain

I spent mornings and middays,
I spent afternoons and evenings,
I spent nights
silently missing you
wherever I was

FEARS

I live in the
constant fear
of losing you
and not being able to say
goodbye

And you don't have
to give it

Don't try
to fool
the one you love
because a second chance
is a gift
not everyone gets

Sorry

say sorry
to yourself

say sorry
and forgive
yourself

forgive yourself
for the times
things got so bad
the only exit you saw
was to hurt
yourself

forgive yourself
for the times
you did not get to
sleep at night
because your thoughts
kept you awake

forgive yourself
for the mornings
you did not want to
wake up
so you stayed in bed
all day long

forgive yourself
for the sake of
yourself

forgive yourself
because you have had
some sleep
since the last insomnia night

forgive yourself
because today
you woke up
at 11 AM instead of
11:30 AM

To my suicidal best friend

Hey you,
I love you
and I know it doesn't make you want to stay
no matter how often I say
I love you
it doesn't take away your bad thoughts
and I wish I could
because you deserve the very best
you're so powerful and strong
you've overcome so much already
and you've been dealing with these thoughts for
the longest time
but darling,
please know,
I will always love you
no matter where you are

To all of you

For those
suffering from depression,
I love you
and I care about you
You are worth it to be here
and to read those words
You are beautiful
and you will survive.
This war inside your head
is not an easy one
but please,
don't let the demons and voices in your head
win
Because no matter what you have been told

You deserve to be here

xxx me

www.ingramcontent.com/pod-product-compliance
Lightning Source LLC
LaVergne TN
LVHW021350200726

843509LV00014B/2774